skate
BOARDING

DK

LONDON, NEW YORK, MUNICH,
MELBOURNE and DELHI

Created by Tall Tree Ltd
Editor Jon Richards
Art Director Ed Simkins
Designer Ben Ruocco

For DK
Senior Designer and Brand Manager Lisa Lanzarini
Publishing Manager Simon Beecroft
Category Publisher Alex Allan
DTP Designer Hanna Ländin
Production Amy Bennett

First published in Great Britain in 2006 by
Dorling Kindersley Limited
80 Strand, London WC2R 0RL
A Penguin Company

06 07 08 09 10 10 9 8 7 6 5 4 3 2 1

A CIP catalogue for this book is available from the British Library.

ISBN-13: 9-78-0-670915-73-6
ISBN-10: 1-4053-1363-3

High-resolution workflow proofed by Media Development and Printing Ltd, UK
Printed and bound in China by L. Rex Printing Co, Ltd

Discover more at
www.dk.com

skate BOARDING

Clive Gifford

Photographer Adam Kola
Illustrator Des Higgins

DK

CONTENTS

6 Introduction

8 Old school skateboarding

12 Wheels

14 Board talk

18 Skate safety

20 Pushing off

22 Tic-tac attack

26 The Ollie

28 Frontside Ollie

30 The Nollie

32 Nollie 180

36 Kickflip

38 Heelflip

40 Boardslide

42 50-50 grind

44 Nose grind

48 Dropping in

50 Pumping

52 On the edge

54 Getting air

56 Skateparks

58 The highest level

60 Glossary

62 Index

64 Acknowledgments

A street move
– jumping down
some steps.

INTRODUCTION

Skateboarding is a really amazing sport. It gives you the **freedom** to cruise around and try out **awesome tricks**. No matter how good you get, there are always new moves to learn and **nail** and different places to ride. Even top skaters find **new challenges** to tackle. This book will get you into skateboarding and help you learn the basics – from **board care** and how to **bail out** when falling to performing your first **Ollie**. It will also show you some of the latest and greatest tricks around.

Street skating lets you use any piece of street **furniture**, from benches and kerbs to steps and rails. Just make sure you're skating in a place where it's **safe** and **legal**!

A vert move – grabbing the board while soaring above the rim of a skatepark bowl.

Me + My Skateboard = Awesome Daryl

Two key flavours of skateboarding are **street** and **vert**. Street sees riders use parts of the urban landscape, like **kerbs**, concrete **slopes** and **handrails**, to try out moves on. Vert skating sees skateboarders use **bowls**, **ramps** and **pipes** to perform spectacular tricks.

Pro legend Tony Hawk pulls a handplant trick at the top of a ramp.

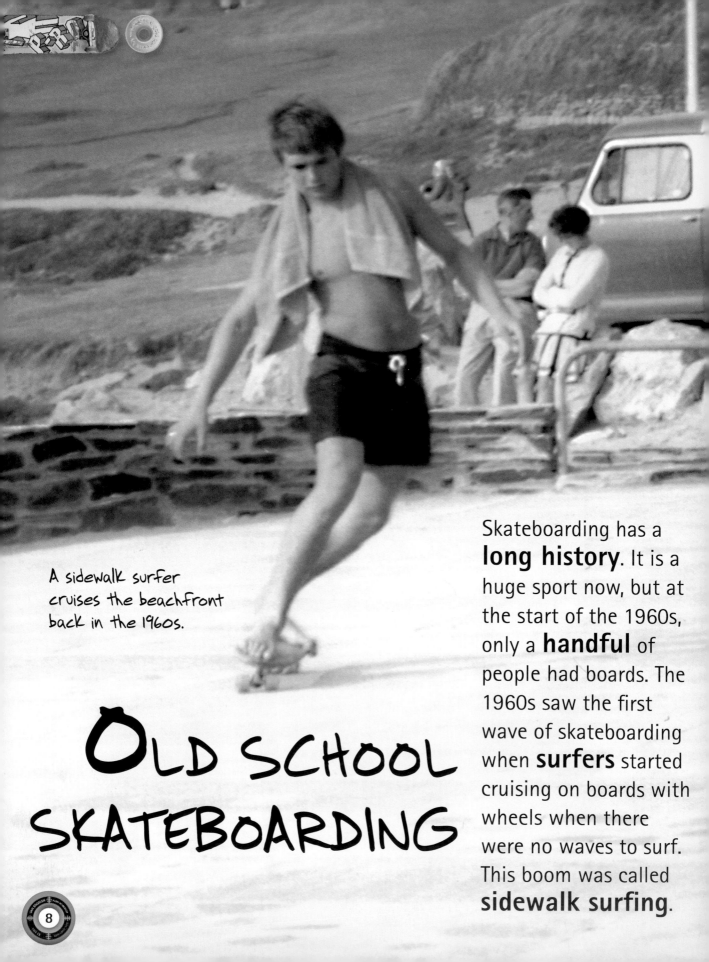

A sidewalk surfer cruises the beachfront back in the 1960s.

OLD SCHOOL SKATEBOARDING

Skateboarding has a **long history**. It is a huge sport now, but at the start of the 1960s, only a **handful** of people had boards. The 1960s saw the first wave of skateboarding when **surfers** started cruising on boards with wheels when there were no waves to surf. This boom was called **sidewalk surfing**.

Empty swimming pools proved the perfect bowls for boarding.

The 1970s saw lots of new **inventions**. These included **urethane** wheels which gripped and rode better, **kicktails** (the curved upwards part of the board at the back) and **wider** skateboards. These helped riders invent lots of new tricks including, in 1978, the Ollie (see pages 26–27).

Skateboard pioneer Tony Alva pulls a great move while pool riding.

There are no rules about what tricks you can and can't do. Invent your own.

Gus

Skateboarding in empty **swimming** pools was popular in the United States in the 1970s. As more and more people owned skateboards, the first concrete **skateparks** were built in America and in Europe. The first opened in 1976.

GETTING ON BOARD

Skateboards come in lots of **different designs**. Your first board is an important buy. An **unsuitable** board might put you off. So, make sure you get advice and a **good quality** board from a specialist **skate shop**.

WHEN I STARTED, I USED SMALLER WHEELS BECAUSE THEY ARE NOT AS FAST.
Taylor

The **hardness** of a skateboard wheel is measured by a device called a **durometer**. The higher the number, the harder the wheel. Softer wheels with a reading of 75-90 are good for **cruising** on roads and rougher ground. Harder wheels with a reading of 95-98 are used in **street** skating.

Wheels come in lots of colourful and great-looking designs.

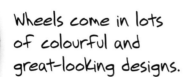

Larger wheels (56 mm or more) are good for cruising and vert riding.

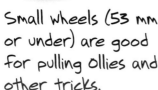

Small wheels (53 mm or under) are good for pulling Ollies and other tricks.

Wheels should run smoothly on their axles. They are held in place by hex nuts.

Between the wheels and the axles are rings called the **bearings**. These contain small steel balls that ensure your wheels turn smoothly.

WHEELS

Wheels are a really important part of your skateboard. They are attached to the **deck** by the metal parts called **trucks**. Good quality trucks are made of aluminium. Wheels come in different sizes and different levels of **hardness**. A good skate shop pro can help choose the right **wheels** for you.

Street skaters use lightweight trucks to help them Ollie up onto rails and ledges.

Keeping the deck of your skateboard clean and dry will help it last.

BOARD TALK

A skateboard has three main parts – the **deck**, the **wheels** and the **trucks**. Decks come in different sizes but most curve upwards at their front, called the **nose**, and the back, called the **tail**. Grip tape is a sandpaper-like material that helps riders to **grip** the board and perform tricks more easily.

Buy a skate tool to help make adjustments.

Trucks are fitted to the **deck** by bolts. You can tighten or loosen the **bolts** a little. Looser bolts make turning easier. But always keep the bolts tight enough so that you cannot undo them with just your **fingers**.

Before **riding**, give your board a quick check. Make sure all the bolts are tight and that the **wheels** run smoothly. If your wheels are worn on their **outer** edge, you can turn them round to make them last a little longer.

You can customise your board with loads of cool stickers.

MY SLICK DECK IS SHINY UNDERNEATH. IT IS AWESOME FOR SLIDING ALONG RAILS!

Gus

STARTING OUT

Ready to ride? Make sure you **begin** to learn skateboarding in a safe place away from **roads** and other **dangers**. Start your skateboarding under the eye of more **experienced** riders. They can help you to learn the basics.

SKATE SAFETY

Skateboarders always fall. So it makes sense to protect yourself. Skating in **safe areas** and never skating on your own will cut down the dangers. So will wearing good quality **safety gear** like knee and elbow pads and helmets. Safety gear lets you skate another day. Learning to **bail** – ways of falling safely – will also help.

The chinstrap of your helmet should always be done up tightly.

KNEE SLIDE

1 As you feel yourself starting to fall, step off the board.

2 As your foot hits the ground, bend your knees and fall onto your pads.

3 Slide until you stop, with your knees together and feet tucked in.

 The skaters featured in this book sometimes skate without their safety gear on. You should always wear full safety gear when performing tricks marked with this symbol.

Some skateparks
insist you wear
safety gear on
ramps and pipes.

NEVER STICK
OUT YOUR ARMS TO
BREAK A FALL OR YOU
MIGHT BREAK THEM!
Gus

Get used to your **stance** on your board while it's not moving. Your **feet** should be across the board, toes pointing slightly forward. Each foot stands just behind a set of **truckbolts**. Choose a **regular** (left foot forward) or **goofy** (right foot forward) stance – whichever feels most natural to you.

PUSHING OFF

1 Pushing off is how you get moving. Place your front foot on the board, just behind the front trucks. Put your rear foot on the ground, next to the board.

2 Kick your rear foot backwards in a smooth movement to get moving. Use your arms to help keep your balance on the board.

3 As your rear foot completes its kick, twist your front foot so that it lies across the board. Bring your back foot onto the board and get into your stance.

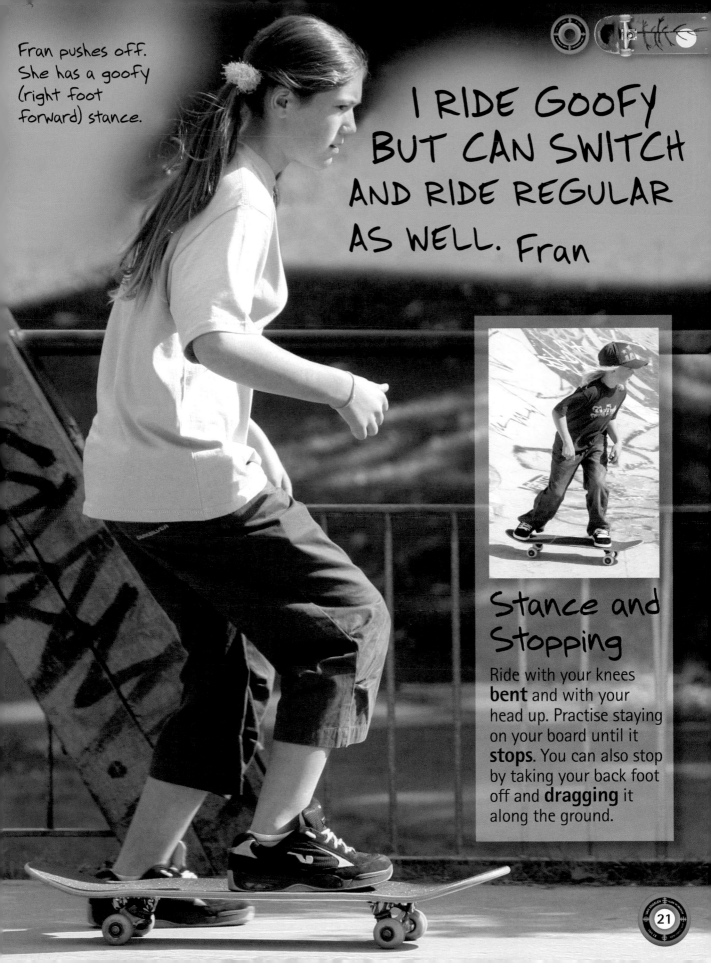

Fran pushes off. She has a goofy (right foot forward) stance.

I RIDE GOOFY BUT CAN SWITCH AND RIDE REGULAR AS WELL. Fran

Stance and Stopping

Ride with your knees **bent** and with your head up. Practise staying on your board until it **stops**. You can also stop by taking your back foot off and **dragging** it along the ground.

1 Move your back foot to the tail and your front foot to the middle.

2 Press gently down on the back of the board and lift the nose. Twist your hips to turn the nose of your board.

TIC-TAC ATTACK

You can perform gentle turns by **leaning** forwards a little and pressing down on the front edge of your board. This is a **frontside** turn. For sharper changes of direction, you can use a **kickturn**. This is where you gently press down on the back of the board, lifting and twisting the nose. A series of kickturns is called a **tic-tac**.

> I USE THE TIC-TAC TO KEEP MOVING ON FLAT GROUND.
>
> Fran

Fran uses her arms for balance as she kickturns. Doing a tic-tac allows her to keep moving forwards.

3 Get some weight over the nose to bring it down. Repeat the move to twist the other way.

4 Repeat kickturning to the left and right to perform a tic-tac.

LEARN AND BURN

Once you are **comfortable** pushing off, **turning** and **stopping**, you're ready to step up for some tricks. The **Ollie** is the most important trick around. Many other moves are based on it. Don't worry if it takes a long time to **master** – learning any trick takes patience. Remember, even pros struggle with **new** tricks. Keep at it.

THE OLLIE

The **Ollie** is the key way of **jumping** with your board without using your hands. Take as long as it needs to get this move **right** as you'll use it to perform lots of other different **tricks**.

1 Get rolling and put your back foot on the tail. Your front foot should be between the middle and the front trucks.

2 Push the tail down hard onto the floor and take all the weight off the front foot. Jump your back foot up and forwards.

Drag your front foot up to the nose as soon as you lift your back foot.

TRY AN OLLIE
WITH THE BOARD NOT MOVING AT FIRST.
Gus

3 Lift your knees as you continue to drag your front foot to the board's nose. The dragging and lifting actions help suck the board up with your jump. Keep your body over the board.

4 Control the board with your feet to level out in the air. Aim to land on all four wheels at the same time. Crouch as you land to absorb the impact.

1 Get into your regular Ollie position but as you start to crouch, wind up your body by turning your shoulders back.

2 As you pull the Ollie, unwind by swinging your arms and shoulders and pulling your front leg around in the direction of your planned turn.

3 As the board levels out in the air, use your feet and legs to help guide the board around its turn. Your back foot should push forwards, your front leg should pull back.

FRONTSIDE OLLIE

Frontside means performing a move with your **chest** facing an obstacle or pointing in the opposite direction to a turn. A **Frontside** Ollie is an Ollie but with a **twist**... a twist through 180 degrees in the air so that you land facing the opposite way.

MAKE SURE YOU TURN THE FULL 180 SO THAT YOU CAN ROLL AWAY WHEN YOU LAND.

GUS

4 Land on all four wheels with the tail of your board now pointing forwards. You should be able to roll away.

Gus pulls his front foot back and pushes his tail foot forwards to complete the full turn.

DON'T SLAM THE NOSE SO THAT YOUR BOARD STOPS DEAD.

Taylor

THE NOLLIE

A Nollie is like an **Ollie** but the other way round. You push the **nose** down to get the tail riding into the air. Start with your **back foot** between the two sets of **truckbolts**. The ball of your front foot should be on the middle of your board's nose.

Sliding his back foot to the tail, Taylor pulls a high Nollie.

1 As you roll forwards, push your front leg and foot down on the nose. This sends the tail of your board up.

2 With the weight off your back foot, drag it up to the tail as you jump up off your front foot. Your board should rise.

3 Let the nose of your board and your front foot rise so that the board levels out. Get your feet planted before landing.

1 Get low as you roll along backside and set up to perform a Nollie move.

2 Snap the nose of your board down nice and hard. As you start to pull the Nollie, twist your hips and shoulders around.

NOLLIE 180

Got your basic **Nollie** nailed well and truly? Then this is the trick for you. The Nollie 180 sees you pull a Nollie and turn **180** degrees in the air to land **frontside**.

I LOVE PULLING NOLLIE 180s OVER STEPS AND OFF LEDGES.
Daryl

3 Stay crouched throughout the turn. This will help you to guide the board and to absorb the impact of landing.

4 Keep turning as you're in mid-air. Your legs and hips guide the board round.

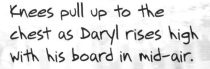

Knees pull up to the chest as Daryl rises high with his board in mid-air.

5 Try not to lean too much and look to nail a landing on all four wheels. Your board should be pointing forwards so you can roll away.

ANOTHER LEVEL

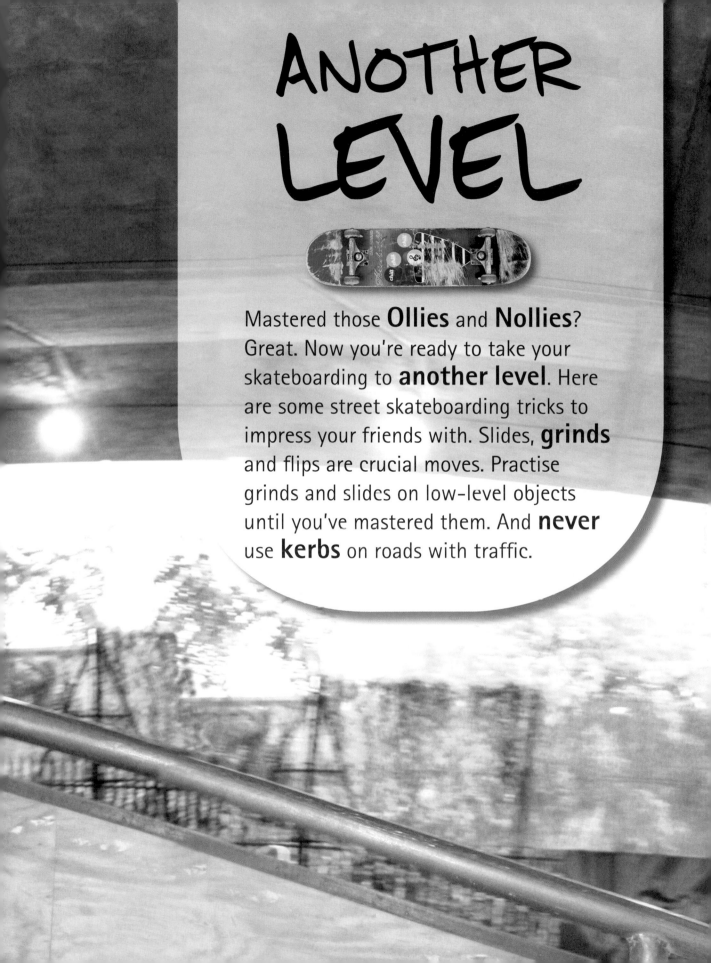

Mastered those **Ollies** and **Nollies**? Great. Now you're ready to take your skateboarding to **another level**. Here are some street skateboarding tricks to impress your friends with. Slides, **grinds** and flips are crucial moves. Practise grinds and slides on low-level objects until you've mastered them. And **never** use **kerbs** on roads with traffic.

KICKFLIP

A kickflip combines an **Ollie** with your board spinning around **360** degrees in the air. It is a great-looking move but will need lots of **patience** to master. Start as you would a regular Ollie but with your front foot **slanted** across and your **heel** hanging off the board.

KEEP WORKING ON THE KICKFLIP UNTIL YOU NAIL IT – IT'S A GREAT MOVE.

Gus

Gus keeps his eye on his board as it spins round in mid-air.

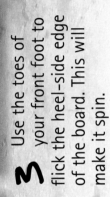

1 Prepare yourself as if you're about to pull an Ollie. Bend your knees and push down on your back foot.

2 As you bring your front foot forwards, it should move across the board towards the heel side.

3 Use the toes of your front foot to flick the heel-side edge of the board. This will make it spin.

4 Catch the board with your feet once it has spun 360 degrees. Bend your knees as you land.

HEELFLIP

Heelflips are similar to **kickflips** except that it is the **heel** of your front foot that flicks the board over. Heelflips and kickflips can be done along the **ground** or, as shown here, off a **jump**.

KEEP THE BOARD
RIGHT UNDER YOUR BODY.
Gus

1 Set up as if you were performing a kickflip but with one crucial difference. Get the toes of your front foot hanging just a little over the edge of the board.

2 Keeping your body straight and holding your head over the board, pop an Ollie. Jump and keep your body directly over the board.

As your front foot kicks off the board, its heel catches the edge.

3 Your front foot kicks diagonally off the board. Its heel catches the front edge of the deck to flip the board so that it spins over.

4 Lift both legs to give the board room to flip over. As soon as you see the top of the deck reappear, get your feet down on the board.

5 With your feet on the board, push it down and land. Bend your knees slightly to absorb the landing and ride away.

THE MORE SPEED YOU USE, THE LONGER YOUR BOARDSLIDE CAN BE. Taylor

1 Approach your target obstacle at a slight angle. Have your feet and body in position to perform an Ollie.

2 Pull an Ollie to get your board above the obstacle. As you travel upwards, turn so that the board will land, straddling the rail.

BOARDSLIDE

A great trick for the street or **skateparks**, boardslides see you travel along a narrow object like a rail using the **underside** of your deck. Start off your first **boardslides** with low-level objects. Skateparks usually feature low **rails** and ledges.

Balance is crucial for a good boardslide. The middle of the board should travel along the rail with the rider's feet an equal distance either side.

3 Land on the middle of the board with knees bent and arms out to help with your balance. Keep the deck level with the ground as you move forwards.

4 When you travel off the end of the obstacle, twist your body to drag the front of your board to point forwards. Land and roll away.

1 Choose a short, low obstacle such as halfway along a kerb in a skatepark. Ride towards it at a moderate speed.

2 As you get close to the obstacle, pull an Ollie and land both of your trucks on top of the edge of the obstacle.

3 As you land, lean back a little and feel the grind of the trucks. Use your arms and body to stay on the edge.

50-50 GRIND

Grinds are moves where you **travel** along narrow objects on your skateboard's **trucks**. The 50-50 grind sees you ride on both trucks along a narrow **kerb** or the top of a ramp.

TRY TO PULL
50-50s FROM FRONTSIDE
AND BACKSIDE POSITIONS.

Taylor

4 As you feel your board slowing, pull a gentle Ollie to get off the edge. Turn your shoulders in the direction you want to come off.

Taylor is about to perform a 50-50 grind in an indoor skatepark.

DON'T PUSH DOWN TOO HARD OR YOUR DECK'S NOSE WILL TOUCH. Daryl

1 Approach the obstacle, such as a kerb or the edge of a ramp, at a good speed. Get ready and then pull an Ollie.

2 Push your front foot past the normal Ollie position ahead of the front truck. The board's tail rises as the nose falls.

3 Aim to land your front trucks. Keep most of your weight over the front of the board. Keep a little weight on the tail to control it.

NOSE GRIND

Grinds come in many **flavours** and can be tried out on lots of different obstacles. A **nose grind** sees contact only with your front truck and the obstacle. The **crooked** version sees the board skewed so that it's not directly over the obstacle. Both are tough moves to nail so be **patient**.

4 When you feel the board slow, pull a Nollie to get off, bending your knees as you land to absorb the impact.

Daryl keeps the board's tail up as he pulls a nose grind.

VERT ALERT

Street is **neat**, but at some time or other, you're going to want to ramp it up and try out **vert** riding. Major skateparks and smaller constructions in local parks often have **bowls**, ramps and half- and quarter-pipes to try out. Watch other, more experienced vert skaters to pick up **useful** tips.

DROPPING IN

You can join a **half-pipe** or a vert ramp from the top using a move called **dropping in**. Standing at the top looking down can be a bit scary at first. Make sure you try out the move on the smallest **ramp** or pipe you can find.

1 Stand on the tail of your board with your back foot. With your weight over the back truck, bring your front foot forwards.

2 Step out confidently with your front foot and place it over the front truck of your board.

I REACH OUT TO MY BOARD'S NOSE WITH MY FRONT ARM. IT MAKES DROPPING IN EASIER!

GUS

3 Crouch over the board and lean slightly forwards as the front of the board starts dropping. Look forward.

4 As the front wheels grip the ramp or pipe, stand a little more upright. You can balance your weight out so that it is over the centre of the board.

Push down with your front foot and get your body weight over it to make dropping in easier.

Taylor switches to fakie stance as he rolls down a half-pipe.

PUMPING

Pumping helps you to build up **speed** on a **half-pipe** without your feet touching the ground. The action takes place as you reach the **transition** – the curving part that joins the horizontal and vertical parts of the half-pipe.

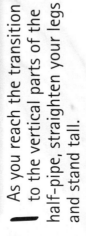

1 As you reach the transition to the vertical parts of the half-pipe, straighten your legs and stand tall.

2 As you go down, crouch and lean into the direction you're heading.

3 Extend your legs as you go up the other side of the half-pipe and switch to fakie stance at the top.

I USE PUMPING TO GET ME ABOVE THE TOP OF THE HALF-PIPE TO PULL AIRS. Taylor

THE AXLE STALL IS A BIT LIKE A 50-50 GRIND WITHOUT MOVING!

Gus

As you get better at **pumping**, you'll reach the top edge, sometimes called the **lip**, of ramps, bowls and half-pipes. You can use this edge to perform a number of **grinds**, slides and other moves such as the axle stall shown here.

ON THE EDGE

1 Ride up the ramp and just before your front truck reaches the edge, perform a kickturn so that your back faces the top of the ramp.

2 Twist your body through 90 degrees as your back truck hits the edge. Lean on your heels to bring the front truck down on the edge as well.

3 You've pulled an axle stall! Now, push on the tail to lift your board's nose up and turn the nose back down the ramp.

Gus is turning out of an axle
stall and shifting his weight onto
his toes. In a moment, he'll be
heading back down the ramp.

DON'T LEAN BACK AS YOU TURN IN THE AIR OR YOU MAY COME OFF YOUR BOARD.

GUS

Getting air (airborne) when vert skateboarding is a real **buzz**. This air move sees you ride up to the top of a **ramp** or half-pipe, get airborne and twist through 180 degrees before **landing** back on the ramp.

GETTING AIR

1 Ride with good speed up the ramp at a slight angle towards the direction you're going to turn. Get into a tucked position with your knees bent.

2 As your board starts to rise above the top edge, twist your body and swing your arms to pull yourself round. You should turn in mid-air.

3 Keep over the board and brace yourself for landing back on the ramp. Lean forward on landing to ride down the ramp or half-pipe.

SKATE PARKS

Skateparks are a great place to **learn** new moves and **improve** ones you can already do. Your first ever visit will be exciting but may also be a little scary. The secret is to take things **gently** and watch others and learn.

A large indoor skatepark in Eindhoven, Netherlands.

Skateparks can be found indoors and outdoors in the centres of towns and cities.

Skateparks come in different **sizes** and types. Smaller and indoor parks often feature wooden ramps and banks. Concrete is used to make half-pipes and large outdoor bowls in which you can pull vert moves. **Snake runs** are twisting and turning downhill courses, while **moguls** are small bumps.

Most skateparks have great **street skating** features such as slide blocks, kerbs and steel rails to practise grinds and **slides** on. They may also have small launch **ramps** which help get you into the air to perform a jump or **aerial** move.

This great-shaped concrete bowl is at Klamath Falls in Oregon, USA.

Skatepark **designers** and builders keep on trying to do something new. In 2005, the **largest** skatepark in the world opened in China. Called the **SMP Skatepark**, it is over 13,000 square metres in area and has a 50-metre wide **vert** ramp.

The HIGHEST LEVEL

At the **highest** level, skateboarders are famous **professionals** – paid to perform. They are sponsored by skate and clothing **companies**, make videos and compete in huge **competitions** such as the X-Games.

Danny Way used a giant ramp to leap the enormous Great Wall of China in 2005.

The world's most famous skateboarder, Tony Hawk, performs a grab in mid-air.

Elissa Steamer slides her board on the way to winning gold at the 11th X-Games in 2005.

Female pro Vanessa Torres in action. Torres won gold at the 2003 X-Games.

Only a handful of **talented** skateboarders ever turn pro. **Most** achieved their dream by practising incredibly hard to learn and nail **tough** new tricks and moves. At all levels, skateboarding is **fun** and a **challenge**. Enjoy it!

Ryan Sheckler was just ten when he became a sponsored skateboarder. He was only 13 when he won the 2003 X-Games street competition.

GLOSSARY

BACKSIDE
When a trick or turn is executed with the skater's back facing the ramp coping or the obstacle.

BAIL
To clear your board safely when a move goes wrong.

COPING
Metal piping or edging fitted to the lip of a ramp or half-pipe. Gives grip.

CROOKED GRIND
Any grind performed where the deck is not directly over the obstacle.

DECK
The wooden area of your skateboard that you stand on.

DROPPING IN
A way of entering a bowl or half-pipe from the top.

FAKIE
Riding your skateboard backwards.

FRONTSIDE
When a trick or turn is performed with the skater's front facing the ramp coping or the obstacle.

GOOFY STANCE
Skating with your right foot forwards.

GRAB
Using your hand or hands to hold the board during a move.

GRIND
A move which involves scraping your skateboard's trucks along an object.

GRIP TAPE
Sandpaper-like material fitted to the top of a deck to give riders more grip.

KICKTURN
To turn your board by shifting the weight to the tail of the board and twisting.

LIP
The top edge of a bowl or ramp.

NOLLIE
Short for a nose ollie.

NOSE
The front of the board.

OLLIE
A move which sees you use your feet to pull the skateboard up into the air.

PUMPING

Moving your bodyweight on your skateboard to build speed in a half-pipe.

QUARTER-PIPE

A quarter section of a pipe that has a curved piece leading to a vertical ramp.

REGULAR STANCE

When you skate with your left foot forwards. Opposite of goofy stance.

SLIDE

A move where the underside of your deck slides along an object.

STREET SKATING

Using street furniture, such as kerbs, benches and steps, to perform tricks.

SWITCH STANCE

Riding your board and performing moves not using your normal stance.

TAIL

The back end of a skateboard.

TIC-TAC

A series of short kickturns performed in a row. It can give a boarder the momentum needed to travel across a flat area.

TRUCKS

The metal attachments bolted to the deck which connect the axles and wheels to the deck.

VERT RAMP

A specially designed ramp for skateboarding with a horizontal area at its top.

VERT SKATING

Performing moves and tricks in a half-pipe or ramp. It usually involves getting air above the rim of the ramp or pipe.

INDEX

aluminium 13
Alva, Tony 9
axles 13, 61
axle stall 52–53

bailing out 6, 18, 60
banks 56
bearings 13
benches 6
board care 6
boardslides 35, 40–41,
 52, 57, 61
bowls 7, 46, 56, 57, 60

decks 13, 14, 15, 39, 40,
 41, 44, 60, 61
dropping in 48–49, 60
durometers 12

falling 18–19
flips 35
frontside ollies 28–29

Great Wall of China
 58

grinds 35, 42, 44, 52,
 57, 60
 50-50 grinds 42–43,
 52
 crooked nose grinds
 44, 60
 nose grinds 44–45
grip tape 14, 60

handrails 7
Hawk, Tony 7, 58
heelflips 38–39
helmets 18
hex nuts 13
history 8–9

kerbs 6, 7, 35, 42, 44,
 57, 61
kickflips 36–37, 38
kicktails 9
kickturns 23, 52, 60,
 61
knee slides 18

ledges 13, 33, 40

moguls 56

Netherlands 56
Nollie 180s 32–33
Nollies 30–31, 32, 35,
 45, 60

Ollies 6, 9, 12, 13, 25,
 26–27, 28, 31, 35, 36,
 37, 38, 40, 42, 43, 44,
 60

pads 18
pipes 7, 19, 48, 49, 61
 half-pipes 46, 48, 50,
 51, 55, 56, 60
 quarter-pipes 46, 61
pumping 50–51, 52, 61
pushing off 20–21

rails 6, 13, 15, 40, 41, 57
ramps 7, 19, 42, 44, 46, 48, 49, 52, 53, 55, 57, 58, 60, 61
    wooden 56
rims 7

safety 18–19
Sheckler, Ryan 59
sidewalk surfing 8
skateparks 7, 9, 19, 40, 42, 43, 46, 56–57
skate shops 10, 13
snake runs 56
stances 20–21
    fakie 50, 60
    goofy 20, 21, 60, 61
    regular 20, 21, 61
Steamer, Elissa 59
steps 6, 32, 61
stopping 21, 25

street furniture 6
street skating 6, 7, 12, 13, 35, 46, 57, 61
surfers 8
swimming pools 9

tic-tac 22–23, 61
Torres, Vanessa 59
trucks 13, 14, 20, 26, 42, 44, 48, 52, 60, 61
truckbolts 20, 31
turns 25
    frontside 23

United States 9, 57

vert skating 7, 12, 46, 55, 61

Way, Danny 58
wheels 12–13, 14, 15, 29, 49, 61

urethane 9

X-Games 58, 59

Acknowledgments

Dorling Kindersley would like to thank:
Daryl, Fran, Gus and Taylor for all their hard work during
the photoshoot.
The people at Meanwhile Gardens Community Association
Nick at the Halfpipe Skateshop, London
Rory and the guys at Bay66 Skatepark, London
Dan and Darren at Shiner Distribution

Picture Credits:
Many thanks to Martin Öhlander for cover photography
and for the skateboard photo on pages 12-13.

All other photographs were taken by Adam Kola, except:
Alamy: Emma Smith/Photofusion 56tl
Courtesy Convic Design: 57bc
Corbis: Al Fuchs/NewSport 46-7, Larry Kasperek/NewSport 59bl,
Quiksilver/DC 58t
Courtesy Dreamland Skateparks, LLC, Oregon: 57tr
Courtesy Keith Folken: 14
Getty Images: Jamie McDonald 58, Christian Petersen 59tl, 59cr,
Kevin Winters 7br
James Hudson: 2tl, 61br, 62t, 63b
Pete Knowles: 8
Kobal Collection: Agi Orsi Productions/Vans Off The Wall/Pat
Darrin 9t/Glen E.Friedman 9b
Quiksilver.com: Boulgakow 57c
Courtesy of Skate One www.skateone.com: 2tr, 12
Every effort has been made to contact the copyright holders and
we apologise in advance for any unintentional omissions. We
would be pleased to insert the appropriate acknowledgments in any
subsequent edition of this publication.

Daryl

Fran

Gus

Taylor